THE IMPERFECTIONS OF US:
A Collection
of
New & Reenvisioned Poems

AUTHOR:

TRICIA MONK, B.A., M.A., M.S.ED

Table of Contents

Page #	Title
1-2.	Table of Contents
3.	Book Dedication
4.	Title Page
5.	Preface: The Perplexity of a Rose
6.	Wavy
7.	Keylock
8.	Camouflage
9.	Descriptive Tales & Caribbean Queen
10.	Character & Expiration Date
11.	Round 2 & To The Crowd
12.	Masterplan
13-14.	Love
15.	Stopwatch
16.	Shelling the Man
17.	Hidden Treasure
18.	One
19.	Baby Blues
20.	The Feeble Light
21-22.	The 35 Year-Old Runaway
23.	A Prisoner's Longing
24.	Pasar Una Noche en Blanco
25.	Evolving Time

26.	Authenticity
27.	Routes
28.	His Pride
29-30.	Body
31.	I Lied: My Truth
32.	Life
33.	Profit-Air
34.	Hollow Manifestations
35.	New York Nights
36-37.	An African-American Bedtime Tale
38.	A Mother's Guide to SEE
39.	~ Note-taking page ~
40.	~ Note-taking page ~
41.	About the Author

Book Dedication

This book is dedicated to, first and foremost, the Lord above, who has guided me through all the amazing and devastating times, as narrated within.

My favorites in the whole world- "SeaShells of Asia." Remember that you are God's Chosen Ones: Be wise, be smart, be beautiful, and know that you are powerful, and will accomplish all your dreams.

Family- Thank you for being my support circle.

Lastly, to all the triumphs, loss, loves, and haters—result in continual motivation!

Self-Published
Copyright © 2024

Nyack, New York
Printed in the United States of America

All rights reserved. No part of this publication may be reproduced, stored in a retrieval system, or transmitted, in any form or by any means, electronic, mechanical, photocopying, recording, or otherwise, without the notarized prior permission of Lead Author, Tricia Monk.

Library of Congress Catalog
Monk, Tricia
The Imperfections of Us: A Collection of Poetry/
2024 Reenvisioned

English Language- Poetry/Free Verse

ISBN: 979-8-9855563-7-7 (Hardback)

ISBN: 979-8-9855563-8-4 (Digital)

Preface:
The Perplexity of a Rose

Where are the flowers?
When shall they arrive?
And–
To whom shall they be delivered?

He, who has symbolized the rose, the lily, and the daffodil,
to emulate love, thought simply.

Simple minded, to reflect something so profound in a detail of accessibility.

God's treasures, are yes, all so divine,
all so intricate,
intimate,
delicate,
all within its complexity.

But, why a rose?
Not a pearl–
Nor a delicacy—,
       but a mere accessible Rose?
Love runneth through the veins of mankind, like water to a hose.
Poet to a muse,
Divinity to righteousness.
Inseparability.
— aligned,
—inclined,
— accompanied.
Love, the running water within our composition.
Love, naturally our being, like a rose to a garden.

A pedal, smooth, as a brush of life—
    your breath upon my cheek.
    the gentlest exchange of two souls.
    The symbolization of purity of a dove unseen
So, with great honor, and humility,
I give you—
your flowers today,
    within these scribes,
      — these murmurs of time
      — rooted in love
      — totality

Wavy

Be my summer place
My place of self reflection
Devotion
Exploration

My summer place
Some place
Where the ocean meets my spirituality
Sways in the water infinitely.
Mind over waves
Masquerading in the consciousness of the moment

The warm mists
Listen to it wist.
Closely and boldly we stand.

Our mind matters.

So, I fully indulge in this phenomenon of existence with persistence
despite turbulence

Food exchanged for thoughts
Clouding my higher self
Survival or ——
Plagued in coverance?

Be my summer place
Freedom
—- interweaving sounds of nature's nurturing motherhood.

Mother me.
Cuddle me in the cusp of your totality
Bring the verbiage to my tongue
Be my summer place.

Keylock

You got my mind on keylock,
Trying to think beyond the average spectrum,
Illusions appearing as solutions,
Finding myself confused, used, and abused.

Your manipulations bring me temporary simulation.

What's your prize for keeping me disguised, disguised from your lies and true ties?

I envision my escape, only resulting in the awareness of my state.
I want out, need a resolution.
This pain is endless, frightening, it's so defying.

Knowing it's not love makes it all the more distressful.

Internal blockade of emotions, restricts the sensations of my keylocked mind.

You're selfish with my freedom,
envious of my potential, and threatened by my strength.
No longer will I sustain my status of being keylocked in your circle of betrayal.

Do you even know your portrayal?

Camouflage

Emotions Derived from Camouflage
I think I love you,
I know I love you.
I love your every way.
The imperfections of your style are all so right.
The distance of your thoughts, identify your true identity.
The mysteriousness of your ways keeps me curious to the hidden you.

I think I love,
I know I love you.
I love your very scent.
Pure Hugo Boss, just cause you're a boss!
Leaving behind the sensations of your presence, only to have me wonder of your latter moves.
Smooth simulations of your aroma; have me dependent on your every appearance.

I think I love you,
I know I love you.
I love your humor; disguising me from the ugly truths of our reality.
Let me remain in this bliss, blissful vibrations of laughter, tenderness, and explorations.

I think I love you,
I know I love you.
I love you till the point it hurts.
Sounding as if the record was played once before, but instead, you're the new lead.
Play, play, and play some more, this sweet melody till the numbness subsides; temporary unconsciousness of this feeling called love.

I think I love you,
I know I love you for sure.

Descriptive Tales

Words can't describe the feelings that I vibe,
Your touch is a never-ending feel, sensation, motion, and tension in my veins.
I want you to stay, divine timing between you and I.
Your words are emotions that surface in my mind.
Repression, digression all extract from the past. Understanding the distance of time, recognizing the faults of life, move fast, but slow, as I recollect the moments.

Caribbean Queen

Away and confused, like, a lighthouse light,
burning during the day, in sunlight's rays,
burnt out by night,
look for a way, to find my way,
which way is that?

Follow my heart's lead, it beats, like the drums
or the sunshine,
I found my Caribbean coast
So close, but so far
wickedly great, so far, the odd and a weirdo,
escaped into bliss,
blindness, innocence, vacations to institutions
work week brunches,

A new wave of punches, punctures stabs at my heart, broke the drum, sun went down, caught a plane, are we done?

Away and confused like a lighthouse,
talking to the waves crashing into it
on the most awkward of days.

Butterfly or colorful caterpillar,
patterns don't exist, no matter how long it appears, it was only a day,
up all night looking for my way!

Character

Your scent, your touch is everlasting, like the words of a favorite book.
Indulging some more, seeking a deeper meaning.
Questing for the captivity of your heart.
Road maps, navigations, all have rerouted.
Your spontaneity is inexplicable, wondrous as to which human trait it replicates.
Mental devotion,
Sole alienation, until I complete my task of identifying your intricate character.

Expiration Date

Flowers,
singers,
sadden faces,
colorless clothes,
jumbled languages,
poems,
speeches,
stylish hair,
musical tones,
bowed heads,
fidgeting fingers,
sobs,
old ages,
minimal young faces,
slugged walks and postures,
forgotten tales,
shortened laughs,
small meals,
watered eyes_____,
I envision my death.

Round 2

I hate that I hate you.
Yeah, I hate you.
I hate everything about you:
Your smile, I'd die for,
Your lips, I yearned to kiss,
Yeah, I hate it all.

Our past relations, I loved, cuz it reminded me of my youth.
Yeah, I hate that too.
I hate that you've made me hate myself.
I hate you, I hate that you've made me hate once again

To The Crowd
Don't get the crowd, for I will and shall upset them,
My thoughts I'm sure are contrary to their votes,
I plan to impact the masses,
My voice is a weapon of destruction.
Conceal it, confine your emotions they aren't welcomed in this world of cattle-ism,

"Speak, speak, let it be heard," "It's written in our rights!" I confer, hearing echoes, as no one is in sight,
Prisoner of my thoughts, individuality got me divided, isolated, desolated,

Okay, Okay, hear, I go again.
You listen closely to refute my pains, ridicule my sacrifices,
How dare thee conjure a false interpretation to fit your flavor?
You selfish bitch, sole being within,

I progress.

My replicated Radical Laryngectomy will ensure you recall these moments.
Be sure not to beg nor plea, for I will return the support provided during my bluntness.
Until that time, project as loud as you may,- I now know, like the rest, you lack true tone.

Masterplan

Is it writer's block, brain freeze,
tall trees, strange leaves,
insane breeds, no pleas!

Seeing things out,
Escort, Cautious!
Don't wanna be dead,
cell floor, nauseous.

Never made it home,
orphan, often…
Thinkin of a Masterplan to get lost in!

Many years muted, dreams, inaudible.
Lonely is so heavy, but light, portable.

Breeze like autumn dew,
sneakers never laced, feelings on my sleeves,
I'm going on my eighth!
Grieved cause I'm peeved,
but stand strong,
porcelain.
Thinking of a Masterplan to get lost in!

Eyes, no pupils,
professors, no pupils,
lessons, no tutors,
but my scruples so truthful!
Cops will shoot you,
system will loot ya.

Suffocation or poison,
way of a snake.
With the weight of the world,
my shoulders should break.

A break from the world,
my shoulders could rest,
with a piece of my coffin,
Thinkin of a Masterplan to get lost in!

Love

My elevated, willful
comprehension of you,
Love,
has deep seeded, extended and
heated, blood!
We used to be tough as fuck,
now we no longer pups, wut
up?

My elevated willful
comprehension of your love,
has deep seeded , extended and
heated,
my sentiments are defeated.
The taste isn't filling,
I'm reluctant to eat it.
Don't agree with this face,
never saw it before,
I equate it with hate!
Sweet turns sour,
who created that fate?

You hate what you loved,
plus loving to hate.
Air tight bliss,
until something escaped .
Maybe in the toilet,
do you equate it to waste?
Wait…

Make a list,
the good and the bad.
The bad goes first,
luggage bag to the purse,
the crabs, all the jerks,
plus the males you dealt with,
your closet is too fragile to
shelf shit.

I need a nurse,
someone alert ,
see symptoms,
someone's hurt,
sweeter than some desserts.

Faulty lines is where we built
our estate.
So, every time I wake, I pray it
doesn't quake.
But, before I sleep, I pray I
don't awake.

I harvest for many seasons,
Mrs. Dash is fucking leaving,
out of business, mental fitness
has murdered itself.
On trial , I'm the only witness.

I don't wanna harbor,
just wanna sail.
I know the price,
want a sale.
The vivid lights are looking
pale.

Follow my words,
arrive at my thoughts.
Check in your heart,
if it's clear, move on Embark!

Just like trees, leave.

Look for the fruits.
Clean through the facts,
get to the roots.

Who rejected, designed
deception coups?
Tied your progress,
the knots of a noose.

Contaminated your keynote,
all your values rewrote,
since the day you met him,
you've been sliding down a ski
slope.

With every problem, there's a
solution.
Cure a symptom,
let the root live-, that's living
ruthless.

Truth is, you've no bite,
you're toothless, can't say shit.
And nothing in your head
matters,
it's just grey shit.

Your mind can't focus,
It strays fast,

running down the sole of your
Asics,
Chasing Love!
Don't try to complicate the
Basics: One plus one doesn't
need notation.
Climb through the hole, or live
in a cage with-,
sorrow and defeat.
No pardons to the weak.

My elevated comprehension is
accurate,
not a product of arrogance, or
happenstance!

Stopwatch

Dedicated, fractionated, confused, wanting this shit to be over.
You can't be serious, got me waiting like a time clock stuck on eternity. Appeals, lawyers, letters, operators, c.o.'s, I'm pissed.
Bitches confirm your stay is temporary.
Annoying the shit out of me, as I realize they are conscious.

Suspended in the past, not seeing the moving cars, years, laughs, people, notions, and experiences.
Bursts of the truth send a frightening roar echoing throughout my veins. Ahhhhhhh! It hurts.

Silent cries, no one wants to listen.
My tale- solely entertainment,
others glance, often pierce me with their gazes.
How the fuck?
What's her deal?
I say nothing, leaving you to their imagination.

I've been slaughtered, someone get the aide.
I'm angry,
What the fuck happened and when?
How the fuck did I land here and why have you captured my mere existence?

You knew of your goal, as you are a one-man team.
Share the plans, let her know.
The ideal survivor, product of a gamble.
Is it too late to cash-out?
        -Fuck…wait there's an understanding.

Shelling the Man

New love,
True love,
Daydream, I stare into the blue love.

My dew love, natural mist,
Saddled my arrogance,
Crashed my conceit!

I'm nauseous, nautical miles,
No porting,
So awesome!

Oh, how the best things in life are free.
Oh, how I wasted so much time investing in "things."
Mutable trends,
Dogmatist friends,
Depreciated life,
Styled with lifestyles of foolhardys'

You're my howsoever,
My Malcolm quote: By Any Means
My scope,
Your intrusion,
Rendered me ineffective.
You're Half-French,
I'm remonstrating against everything I thought or knew.
Can you repatriate me- to the place I'm from?

I'm stranded, lost,
At a cross between my experiential fact bank, and my inability to match mate!

Balancing means,
Denuding or tipping,
My gauntlet covered bands,
Finding answers in the sands of a clogged hour glass.

I'd follow a yenta, If she spewed out hope, To cope with my---New Love, True Love, Daydream, I stare into the blue love,
Cream of my dew,
Ahhh, Love

Hidden Treasure

Disappointment after disappointment, wondering how to handle it well,
A professional failure- is the accomplishments I attain.
Minimum deceptive solutions succumb to my inner being in so many ways.
Placing real blame on the causes of my errors,
Deterrence- from the truth leads me further from actualization.

Mistaken identity- I'm no longer the woman I used to be.
Distorted values, angry motivates, false personas, torn friendships, distant, disillusioned.

Confidence has subsided, yearning to blend in the shadows.
The star of a discontinued sitcom,
Laughing at the woman I once was, as I imprinted my own footprints.
Follow them not,
Useless to the wise woman of defiance.
Pave the way for the young to emulate, never wanting your name to be mentioned in shame, followed by "however" conjunctions.

Let it stand in solitary, never relying on fortunes to carry the burden of fame.
I have devastated the temple, not acknowledging the disciples to come.
I beg of thee to find what's real, know its worth---beneath the piles of life's burdens, shield your chastity:
IT is tamed, waiting for your discovery,
A true gem.

One

Winners sometimes lose,
But losers never win a thing!
You will win, you will fly,
I gave you wings.

The chance to see marigolds,
Free to be any role, achieve any goal,
The world is yours.
The chance for me to shower you,
My only girl.

Stand tall
Tower through every road.
Many things will be said,
Several things will be heard,
Within you is the truth when the world is absurd.
I can't put everything in words,
Or explain the nerve,
You have to just take and learn.

I waited for you,
And weighted by you, even hated for you.
I'll separate, and dedicate myself to your delicate needs.

Prepare you for the sunny people, cold shoulders, and people that breeze.
Prepare you for the Seas, and introduce you to the deserts.
When you struggle through the seasons, know it's just some weather.

The sun's little flower,
No matter how bad it seems,
It's only twenty-four hours.

- Daddy

Baby Blues

How do I handle sickness?
        Must I grapple cough?
Try to laugh it off?
        Or, stand by in shame?

You get needles,
        I cry in pain.

Please give me the name,
        Of whoever never got sick.

And, please show me the parents who had no medical trips.

The Feeble Light

Seeing the changes evolve in sight is so devastating. Never expecting the worst- now living its reality.

Motivation to transcend evaporated like the thin summer breeze we once enjoyed.

The idea of sitting on the benches, rehearsing the name of our unborn child is as foreign as the thought of you putting the green weeds and blunt wrap to your lips.

Seeing the changes got me tripping. Matter of fact, I've fallen; Not wanting to rise only to be approached with the life that has abandoned me, forsaken me for the envious "green" ways of my past.

Please allow me the chance to retract. I promise I've learned:
To listen to my elders,
Use mistakes as lessons,
Take life in healthy strides,
Create a path to be followed- oppose to avoided.

Despite the apparent mess of inevitable change, I sit in sorrow--
seeing, ignoring, - the changes.

I'm shattered, the pieces off at sea. How will I be repaired? Yearning for assistance,
in a resisting manner, left to negotiate my make-up for reinvention.

He has lost. Is lost. Yet guiding us.
Will they be found?

The 35 Year-Old Runaway

The black man is missing once more.

Where are the Toussaints, and Dessalines to shake their heads in disgrace?
Protecting a nation, race for mankind.
Cutting heads with swords to save the purity of the black women's natural treasures.
Pure land, pure morals.
The black man was present more than ever.

Showing his strength,
an arm of iron,
tongue of steel,
strike of fire,
The black man was a presence to be in.

Negotiations, compliments, threats, and treachery, leading to
the victory of freedom.
The black man,
    ever so present.

So proud were mothers, daughters, wives, and aunts,
standing to see the black man's stride,
standing tall for his beliefs, his nation, his heritage, his future-
the black man was strong.

Too strong for his opponents, only to be fooled.
Too wise and confident for his own good.

Oh, how strong was he.

Body builds of lust.
Desiring the black man was an inevitable cause.
His family unit remained solid, setting the standards for his time.

The black man was present, I felt his worth.
Interweaving everlasting treaties in the land's quilt work.
Demanding listeners and standing ovations.
Yeah, the black man was strong.

His strength didn't vanish at sea, with false intentions; it coasted the sea, spreading throughout the nations of black men, reaching the Quakers' land.

The black man's toils didn't go unanswered.
He sacrificed but remained strong-

Until that day he held the white flag, surrendering himself, family, daughters, sons, brothers, and mothers.

The black man was defeated.

His strength undone,
Coined-" the 35 year old runaway" by the single mother of two

A Prisoner's Longing

Boon are your handcuffs,
On my wrist,
My wrist would be slit,
If you let me go.

Flow out every drip,
No safety valve switch.
Dead to my peers,
Dead to my fears, all have confirmed now.
Dead to and through years, which way is home now?

No watch,
No clock,
Call and tell me of the times I left at airports, beaches, at bars, and weekends afar.
All I know is weekend enjoyments are far.

Damn! I miss my kids.
Tickle their ribs,
Pickle their brain with thoughts of me home.
Daddy in the room, mom in the kitchen,
Or daddy in the kitchen, mom always bitchin.
Our spice of life,
Season our own way.
Things I miss,
I miss them all day.

Pasar Una Noche en Blanco

Many nights,
I toss and turn
for a small moment of sleep!

Linked and looped through dimensions.
I blink!

Eyes adjust to the darkness,
to lighten the confusion.
Thinking convoluted,
works great, means straight, within my circuitous mind.

Seasoned and fried,
in the ghetto's kitchen,
pour from poverty's pot!
To hot to consume,
too sick to plague!

Cleaned in the tub, where misery bathes.
I pray,
to a calendar,
asking for better days.

I opened every door and stoked the devil's maze.
Amazed,
this page of life is invisible ink.
It riddles my reach,
as my ability leaks,
out of my pores and my heart pours out in heaps.
Many hours I toss and turn for just a moment of some sleep!

Evolving Time

Waiting for time to evolve,
These moments are memories soon to dissolve. Waiting patiently, unable to precisely perceive the motions at hand. Indivisibly biased is the truth of the present. Baby mothers, single fathers, wed-locked children, chasing dick, a constant strive. When will the barrel break, and time evolve?

Restless in "saving every cent." The Haitian Dream, turned to the American Dream, and retracted back to my Deferred Dream. I'm dried up, washed up, tired of hoping and waiting for him to evolve. Evolve into the man of my imagination, the man who she begs for mercy. Evolve already.

You read this and speculate my inner thoughts. Don't. I speak dem clearly. I'm saddened, angered, betrayed, hated, and revengeful of time. I want it to move s-l-o-w-l-y during the good times, and Evolve! during times as such.

Young kids, beating on each other--- females, males, and the elder. I'm nervous, having to build a shield, yielding, everyone to stay away. The hard exterior has converted into my interior. A self-made beast, stay away! Until time evolves, I am me. Tongue sharper than any machete he can find in the remote areas of Les Cayes. The pains of life have raised me. Battered women, men's fist, unseen tears---escape me! leave my mind to itself. Would –you—please- evolve?

Evolve to the unknown. Evolve to distant lands of luxury, beauty, payments, and folklores. Evolve to my ideal utopia. Endless pleasure, familiar faces, and time at our disposal. Let it not be in death for one to know his or her true worth. Know that time has waited and evolved for you solely. Understand that time of deception leads to appreciation of authenticity. Until then… I patiently wait, loudly, for Time to Evolve.

Authenticity

Give me a neighborhood decorated with graffiti, because it means inspirations are amidst

Give me hair salons filled with different dialects, it keeps my roots alive

Give me culture inspired restaurants, because it lets me know my dreams may actualize.

Give me the corner fights; they let me know self-pride still exists.
Give me the unique extensions, as I resemble my African tribes.
Give me a curvy body, they let me know I'm childbearing.
Give me a tongue sharper than a machete, lets you know not to fuck with me.

Routes

Where do I find the strength to go on?
Been defeated so many times,
Conquered yet I still walk.
My legs and rhythm automatically beating to their own drum.
I know it's dumb, rhetorical to wonder the motivation, but I am curious, suspicious of the human mind.

Told to seat down, to no longer make a sound.
Becoming an outer shell of my true identity, never wanting to display my inner strength I fear of your approval.
Where do my thoughts find the avenue to thrive, aspire, and explore?
The road is dusted, far from paved, understanding the trails it has taken to land me here.
Yet in great distraught with struggles that still bear.

When will my heart synch with my soul? When will my destiny follow my passions? When will I bear contentment? Backwards roller coaster ride got me tripping. I know this isn't my path. It doesn't feel right, too uneasy to know where to sit.

I'm visiting different stations, never finding my seat.
Tickets half-purchased, wanting to explore different routes.
Walking through, straight through.
You tried.
Tried aggressively to defeat me.

My heart, my legs, my soul, beat to their own original drum.
The drum of my ancestors. The drums of Africa. The drums of warriors, the ones that made their way, defined it, and past it on for inheritance.

I'm more than the physical, I'm all I know nothing of. So, for you whom tries to conceal me, STOP! I will succeed.
Succeed all your doubts and all my dreams.
I know where I'm coming from, so the going is even easier.

Thanks to God.
~My conscience

HIS PRIDE

HE made me big, proud, and Black
To bear a life of turmoil, led by persuasion,
HE made me big, proud, and Black.

I sit often contemplating HIS motives of delivering his child into poverty, sorrow, and shear madness. But, my eyes see, never to touch. My ears hear, only to learn and recollect. My heart pumps fear- fear for me, them, they, us. I'm fearful daily, smile rarely.

HE made me big, proud, and Black

Black like the inhabitants of the lonely Caribbean Sea, holding the dreams, stories, and defeats of many. Black like the imprints of the historical accounts, of the masses, masses of cattle cargo Africans- chained, whipped, ignored, voiceless in the dark nights of their Blackness. An empty vessel, no see-through, pointless, like the life so many live.

HE made me big, proud, and Black

Big, big like the towers that rule the streets, and alleyways of Manhattan. Like the King of the Highways. Big. Hips designed to take in a true black man, with all his gifts. Big. Big to bear the fruits of my labor. Big. Big to defeat the envious thoughts and mutters that fill a room of my presence.

He made me big, proud, and Black.

So, when the world requests a big proud beautiful Black woman to bow her head of disgrace, stand taller than the towers, put your hands on those curvious hips, and whine, whine, whine, whine like the island girls of the Caribbean, forgetting about all the sorrows of the time. Enjoy yourself, the moment of mere existence.

He made you big, proud, and Black.
Amen

Body

I had a dream one December
I was able to converse with my body, I remember.

Asking eyes if they've seen love
And-
If water is thicker than blood?

Water said,"Without me blood couldn't sail."

I asked heart about love, he said go to mind.
Mind was distracted and asked for some time.

So I asked touch if it felt love,
"Maybe," he said.
"Maybe when I was innocent...a baby."

He was unsure, Maybe thought I said Pure.
I repeated the question, he said "Awaken brain from snore."

Leaving touch, going to brain, where he sent me.
There was holes and patches in this area called memory.

The sky, there, gray, clouded with calm.
I asked, "Are you brain?" Out his mouth came a fog.

It lingered in the air of my personal space.
His mechanical voice said "You're at the right place."

"I heard your question because I record everything different from Mind, who puts importance on things."
"Unfortunately for you, I've recorded various answers, I've heard love in song and various anthems."

"Smelled it behind closed doors, as you were gasping the power, sweat and sweet air--- love was passion."

"Tasted it at those Sunday church dinners."
Best dish award, Love was the winner.

"Seen in the likes of your wife,"
"She gave you her life to ease your strife."

"Before this dream ends, here's a question for you…"
"What makes love so confusing for you?"

I said, "I thought something solid couldn't have melted."
"Now it's hard to believe I have ever felt it."

"You deal with what you're dealt with, because you heard, tasted, seen, and smelled love."

I awoke, called to tell my wife about my nightmare last night. I said that my whole body said that I'm in love with my wife.

I Lied: My Truth

The first time I lied, was back in the day.
See, beatings made me cry, I had to find a way.

Nobody appeared to care, as long as it didn't hear THEM.
Everything was cool, and everyone was friends.

I lied about my home, its address and all.
Made people believe they were better, but I was better at ball.

I lied about my family. My existence in deadweight-- ROCK LAND.
Really, I'm Harlem, Rockland only-- via an ugly adoption.

Told rappers they were good, though really trash.
Made the suburban kids think they were tough, yet I knew they were ass.

I'd fake, then throw a punch, then shout "one-on-one!"
I did it often, to avoid getting jumped.

My friends taught me voodoo, during Catholic School Days
One day I said, "I'm God." They all went berserk.

Told mom, I loved her, never really did.
I never felt love until I hugged my first true kid.

I'm loud, and reckless. Inside I'm really shy.
I wait, and calculate to seize the perfect time.

I make future plans, but don't wanna live another day.
I expand my mind, but live the same way.

You lie to yourself at night, and call'em dreams.
Our difference is operation, design, and scheme.

Hear my truth within.

LIFE

Scorched by stress, dead hair follicles.
    Life , tastes like a straight shot,
of Russian water,
    historically distilled,
vitriol within the mouth,
    violently washing soft tissue,
of the freshmen and un-oddy.

    Life, feels like wrinkles on young faces,
chiseled by worriment,
    helpless, unhopeful,
visibly beaten between forbearance and lust,
    violently starving the vigor,
of the guilty and innocent.

    Life, smells like air-proofed despair a,
fire on flesh,
    no smoke,
unbathed urban borough'd cocktail,
    violently mixing the cultures,
of the disobedient and civics.

    Life, looks like Manfred on Jungfrau,
like optional suicide,
    snow squalled,
vie Vying for daily recrudesce,
    violently staying alive,
of the pitiful and wild.

    Life, sounds like a steel hell,
cold steel bars,
    keys, echos
inaudible screams atop lungs,
    violent kicks, stomps, punches,
of the body and soul,

Black Men and Women wither in the way of the old.

Profit-Air

Unreasonable profits have been made,
Through an enslaved sweaty wage.
Through caged intellectual capacity,
The swallowing process of capitalization,
Sickened at the sigh, a choking profiteer.

Choking on profit, and the profundities of his profit center.
Deficient in decency,
From first endorsement to position of regency.
The inner-city, poor, blinded by allure, and binded in stores.
Hoping to fly high, make a mark, a stamp, finish the fifty, a trophy, or a ring.

But lacing up his sneakers is like building Sing-Sing!
But, lace up your sneakers,
And pray for the jackpot,
Cause he prays your ass gets locked up in a cement box.
And, remember, he's a champ,
Champions never lose.

If you want to win, don't buy his shoes.

Retreat.

Don't attend his camps, his functions,
And don't wear his clothes.

His goals are unlike yours,
He's a defense contractor,--that likes wars.
He's the gun in the knife fight,
The drop of poison in the Christmas dinner, matterfact —the hard price!
Clandestine!
The chauffeur to a prison cell,
A blackface living well,
Fooling those who supported'em, and still don't give a hell!
What's lower than the cost to make his goods?
The price of his soul,

Black as if a piece of coal had cancerous lungs.
Black like the mask at the opera on the phantoms' face.
Blacker than Jim Crow's legacy.
Blacker than the inner-city.
Blacker than a dark night in jail.
Profiteer gambling to make money never fails!

Hollow Manifestations

Take everything that you hear,
    Set it on fire!
Go online, and call the Pope, Prez, or Priest a liar: Press Send.
Argue with everyone--all your friends,
    Sue both your parents,
Ignore what's apparent,
    Unleash all beliefs and let it blend.
Create your own world,
    Name it,
Take a hundred selfies a day,
    Be famous.
When things go bad,
    Blame it, —-on your past!
Be heard, not seen.
Text, don't speak.
Speak what you hear, not what you see.
Be that cutting edge thing,
    Live your 20's theme.
That image silver screen,
The female– angry, awkward, and curvy.
The envied male,
Use each word, get'em jealous.
Be the empty-headed human ,
Be thin-skinned, easily stirred like, starved boxed lion,
Sentimental when technology is on, though dry crying.
Find a lane for your brain,
And let go.

Embrace these Hollow Manifestations.

New York Nights

Nights in New York are cold
     bundle up, it's going to be a real one.

Your eyes gotta stay woke, cause niggas will take you for a joke,
     take you for that ride,
     may end up losing ya life.

Nights in New York are cold
     bundle up, it's going to be a real one.

Night terrors
     leaving chills
     running through ya spine;

The realities we hear outside—
     Mother's aborting newborns in the dumpsters,
     Alleyways
         Brothers, Fathers, Sons, and Uncles, losing their lives —
           forced into contemporary slavery.

Nights in New York are cold,
     —-- bundle up, it's going to be a real one.

Thinking of a move.
Mind spinning, hoping for a better chance.
RIP the "New York" label off,
     —- looking towards a lighter coat, lighter load.

Nights in New York are cold, got my mind spinning.
     Niggas grinding for self.
     The realest state got the most heart to leave you floating dolo.

Nights in New York are cold
     —bundle up, it's going to be a real one.

An African-American Bedtime Tale

An African-American Bedtime Tale

Red, burgundy, or a plain tee shirt? Which color should I wear? "I want the crowd in awe upon my entrance.

Iron,
iron-board,
starch,
spray the cologne, for the night must start.

"Pick out your favorite book," "not too long, for it's bedtime."
Princess, sorcerers, and Princes-to-the-rescue.

Friday nights looking for a parking spot
on the busy streets,
 lights,
bumpers,
honks.
Right.
Next to the spot,
—- oh how ideal.

"Mommy, may I please have some milk? I believe I've become thirsty just after using the bathroom, and oh, after the milk, before the story, I need to get my favorite teddy to join."
Patiently waiting for the tasks of the night to unfold, prior to the end in sight.

Out the whip,
"Is that him? He's here, he's here."
Slow walks in search of familiar faces,
        —- and faces to place on reserve.
        "What's up?"
        "What's good?"
        "chilling, chilling."

"Alright girls, off to bed."

Warm tucks and kisses, assuring that the night's darkness is only in the temporary presence, as colorful dreams will be sure to surpass.
Pick up the final toys,
put clothes away,
clean the kitchen and bathroom before the night's end.

"This is my tune!"
Dances,
drinks,
tugs,
—- and air kisses, in the waves of the night.
Playing cat and mouse for the few hours that remain.

All the labors of the house, now done.

Shower,
perfumes,
lingerie.
Awaiting his cumming, as she silently drifts to sleep.

"Daddy's home" — 7am.
Mommy awakes to prepare breakfast, and hopes to one night–
 get dressed,
feel beautiful,
and mistily enjoy the night lights,
replicating her husband.

She whispers in their ear–
> "Daddy is home from work, he's sorry he missed our bedtime tale."

A Mother's Guide to SEE

Loving her is mandatory.
She requires time, and space.
My little ocean-wide, mind and heart.
She demands her respect, though portraying a tiny vessel.
She defines, and defies fierceness, making a mockery of the term.

Expanding your realm of reverence, results from her company,

In all—
I yearn to deliver my zest, wisdom, and love to her.
Protection from the bare arms of others— mere strangers.

Walk through life the way you are.

Your own mother tirelessly tries to shape you,
Change you,
Train you,
     According to her liking;
     You resist, smart beyond your years.

Be you. Never silenced, never stereotyped, but immortalized.

Stay in health.
Take genuine lite breaths, from the challenges and accomplishments of life.
Surface;
Face your SEA with dominance.
Tell the world your presence is inevitable.
See the Sea abound.

About the Author
Tricia Monk
Writer, Poet, and Entrepreneur

Tricia Monk holds two Master degrees from Mercy University in English Literature, and a Masters in Educational Leadership with Distinction. Tricia Monk attends the University of Rochester's Warner School, Ed.D program in Higher Education Administration, and holds a NYS Professional Teaching Certificate in English 7-12.Tricia Monk has taught English, as an adjunct, at several NYS Universities & Colleges. .

Tricia Monk also has published two poetry books, and two more being released December 2024. Her poetry speaks to vulnerability, self empowerment, women empowerment, community, mass incarceration, trauma, healing, the human experience, and the black experience. Tricia's works represent in its full extent—the complexity, and evolution of both the earthly realm and spiritual realms.

Tricia's first nonfiction text- book #3, is a literary thesis that analyzes the causes of the mass migration of Caribbean people.

A New York Native to the core. Tricia is a former member of NYSED Blue Ribbon Commission Advisory Committee. Member of Sigma Tau Delta- International English Honor Society (since 2007–), amongst several other committees, groups, and organizations.

***

Media Coverage

"Spoken word albums often fly under the radar in the music industry, but **Tricia Monk…** demands attention and deserves the spotlight" (WME MUSIC NEWS 11/06/24).

"Monk's authentic storytelling and mesmerizing flow create an intimate atmosphere that draws the audience into her world of emotions and experiences" (WME MUSIC NEWS 11/06/24).

"Tricia Monk's journey as an artist is deeply rooted in her upbringing and lifelong love for writing" (WME MUSIC NEWS 11/06/24).

"…to Maya Angelou and Virginia Woolf, demonstrating her appreciation for authenticity and the power of words to convey complex experiences and emotions" (WME MUSIC NEWS 11/06/24).

"Tricia Monk's … [writings] … serves as a reminder that in a world often dominated by noise and distraction, there's immense power in stripping away the excess and speaking directly from the heart. Her words challenge us to embrace our own authenticity, to explore our deepest emotions without fear, and to recognize the beauty in our shared human experiences" (WME MUSIC NEWS 11/06/24).

Lustful Desires: Tricia Monk's Poetic Symphony of Love and Authenticity

Echoes of Passion: Tricia Monk's 'Lustful Desires' Redefines Spoken Word

LUSTFUL DESIRES: A JOURNEY OF AUTHENTICITY AND LOVE THROUGH SPOKEN WORD AND MUSIC

A Poetic Symphony of Love and Passion – "Lustful Desires" by Tricia Monk

www.ingramcontent.com/pod-product-compliance
Lightning Source LLC
Chambersburg PA
CBHW050520100526
44581CB00001B/49